21

The "Faith in Action" Series
General Editors: Geoffrey Hanks and
David Wallington

D1825232

THE SECRET ROOM

THE STORY OF CORRIE TEN BOOM

David Wallington

RELIGIOUS AND MORAL EDUCATION PRESS
An Imprint of Arnold-Wheaton

Religious and Moral Education Press
An Imprint of Arnold-Wheaton
Hennock Road, Exeter EX2 8RP

Pergamon Press Ltd
Headington Hill Hall, Oxford OX3 0BW

Pergamon Press Inc.
Maxwell House, Fairview Park, Elmsford, New York 10523

Pergamon Press Canada Ltd
Suite 104, 150 Consumers Road, Willowdale, Ontario M2J 1P9

Pergamon Press (Australia) Pty Ltd
P.O. Box 544, Potts Point, N.S.W. 2011

Pergamon Press GmbH
Hammerweg 6, D-6242 Kronberg, Federal Republic of Germany

Photographs are reproduced by courtesy of Miss Corrie ten Boom (pp. 12, 23 top), Stichting Uitzicht (p. 23 bottom) and World Wide Pictures (pp. 2, 9, 17). Cover illustration by Gary Long.

First published 1981

Reprinted 1982, 1984, 1986

Printed in Great Britain by A. Wheaton & Co. Ltd, Exeter

ISBN 0 08-026415-8 non net
ISBN 0 08-026416-6 net

THE SECRET ROOM

The Story of Corrie ten Boom

"You need not fear," said the Dutch Prime Minister over the radio. "We shall not be attacked by any of the countries fighting in this war. They have promised this."

Father ten Boom suddenly turned off the radio. His two daughters, Corrie and Betsie, looked up in surprise.

"The Prime Minister is wrong," said the old watchmaker. "There will be war. Germany will attack us and we shall be defeated."

That night Corrie and Betsie woke up to the sound of explosions. Hitler had suddenly attacked the peace-loving country of Holland without warning. The Dutch army fought bravely for five days, but they had no chance against Hitler's army and air force.

Gradually life changed for the old watchmaker and his family. The streets of Haarlem, the Dutch town where they lived, were filled with German soldiers. No one could buy food unless they had a ration card. Dutch newspapers were stopped. All radio sets had to be given up (although the ten Boom family secretly kept one). Then there was the "curfew", which meant that no one was allowed on the

German soldiers confiscating radio sets (still from The Hiding Place)

streets after a certain time. At first this was fairly late, but gradually it became earlier and earlier, until at last curfew was at six o'clock in the evening.

This meant that Corrie had to close down all her girls' clubs, which she had run for nearly twenty years. These had been started for girls of 12–18 years, and included activities like gymnastics, music, walking and camping. But in the midst of all the fun, Corrie had taken time to teach the girls that God loved them, and that they could always turn to Him in prayer.

She also ran a club for mentally handicapped young people, and she found that many of them really understood when she told them of God's love.

Now all this had to end. Corrie was glad she had taught the girls more than how to enjoy themselves. During the terrible years that followed, many of them found real strength from the faith in God that they had learned from Corrie.

The Star of David

Soon worse things happened. One Sunday afternoon, all the young men out on the streets were rounded up by German soldiers and sent to Germany as slave factory-workers. Some were never seen again. From that time onwards, young Dutchmen had to go about secretly or stay in hiding.

The German soldiers also began to smash the windows of shops owned by Jewish people and steal the goods inside. Sometimes the Jewish shopkeepers and their families disappeared as well. At the time, no one knew what happened to them. Now we know that Hitler and the Nazis murdered over six million Jews in Europe.

One day there was an order for all the Jewish people in Holland to report to the police. They were told that they must wear a bright yellow star, the "Star of David", on their clothes, wherever they went. The Jews had always been proud of this sign, but now it had become a label that set them apart from other people.

The ten Boom family were very sad about this. They loved the Jewish people because the Bible says that they are God's "chosen people". Jesus Himself was a Jew, and most of the Bible has come to us through the Jews.

Father ten Boom also had a son, called Willem. Willem was a church minister, and had worked with Jewish people for a long time. He had a large house in Hilversum for Jews who had escaped from Hitler's Germany before the war. Now he had to find safer places for them to live.

On a rainy day in November 1941, some German

soldiers broke into a fur shop across the road from the ten Boom home. It was owned by a Jew called Mr Weil. The soldiers smashed the windows and took all the furs. Then they threw Mr Weil's clothes into the street.

Corrie ran outside and brought Mr Weil into their home above the watch shop. He told them that his wife was staying with friends in Amsterdam. It was clear that Mr and Mrs Weil could not go back to their home.

As they thought about the problem, Corrie and her sister Betsie both felt they must ask their brother Willem what they should do. Corrie went to his home in Hilversum that afternoon. Willem was out, but his twenty-two-year-old son, Kik, was in. Corrie explained the problem.

"Tell Mr Weil to be ready as soon as it's dark," said Kik.

That evening at nine o'clock Kik rapped on the door, and led Mr Weil away into the dark.

About two weeks later, Corrie met Kik again. She asked where he had taken Mr Weil.

"If you are going to work with the 'underground', Aunt Corrie, then you must learn not to ask questions," he answered with a smile.

Soon other Jewish people came to the ten Boom home asking for help. Although the family knew it was dangerous, they were all agreed that they must help. They had several spare rooms in the old house, but it was only a hundred yards from Haarlem Police Station! Besides, there was the problem of getting food for people who had no ration cards.

The Dutch underground

Corrie went to talk things over with her brother Willem, but he could not help. He already had so many people who needed hiding-places that he could not deal with any more.

The ten Booms' house in Haarlem

"You will need ration cards as well as places to hide your Jewish friends," he said. "You will have to find your own supply."

On her way back to Haarlem, Corrie thought hard. How could she get ration cards? How could she find families who were willing to risk hiding a Jewish person? She began to pray. As she did so, a name flashed into her mind – Fred Koornstra. His daughter used to belong to one of Corrie's girls' clubs. Yes, didn't he work in the office where ration cards were issued? But would he help? Could he be trusted? Again she prayed, and then felt certain that she should go and see him.

That evening she called on Fred. Could he help?

"Quite impossible," he replied. "Those cards are counted over and over again. There is no way I could take any – unless there was a robbery! Perhaps I know the very man...."

"Don't tell me any more," said Corrie. "It wouldn't be safe."

A few days later Fred Koornstra called at the watch shop. He had a black eye and some bruises. The "robbery" had been very true to life! But he had the ration cards.

Soon Corrie realised that through her girls' clubs, and through the watch shop, she knew half the people in Haarlem. Each time she needed to ask someone for help, she prayed, and then she seemed to know whether it would be safe or not. This was important, for many Dutch people did not want to run the risk, and some were actually helping the Germans in return for more money and food, and good jobs.

One evening Kik took Corrie to a big house in Haarlem to meet a group of Dutch "underground" workers. These people worked secretly against the Germans to help the Allies (countries like Britain and France who fought on the same side as Holland in the Second World War). If a British aeroplane was shot down by the Germans, the underground workers tried to rescue the pilot. If they found out about a train carrying ammunition meant for the Germans, they blew up the train. If Dutch people were arrested, they tried to free them.

Corrie recognised an old friend of her father's among the underground workers. The ten Booms called him Pickwick because he reminded them of a picture of a character in Charles Dickens' *Pickwick Papers*.

Pickwick told the others that Corrie was helping the Jews in Haarlem, and one by one they told her how they could help.

"I can get you false identification papers," said one.

"I can get you an official government car, if you need one," said another.

Then she met an oldish man with a wispy beard. He turned out to be an architect.

"This is Mr Smit," said Pickwick. (Of course this was not his real name. "Smit", like "Smith" in England, is a very common name in Holland, and it was safer for underground workers to be called Smit!)

"What you need," said Mr Smit, "is a secret room in your home, in case the Gestapo raid your house looking for Jews. I will come and visit you to arrange it." (The Gestapo were the hated German police.)

The secret room

"This is a perfect house for a secret room," said Mr Smit when he came. The ten Boom home was a very old house, with all kinds of unexpected corners and spaces in it.

"The room should be as high up as possible, to give your

people time to hide if there is a raid," he said. In fact he chose Corrie's own little room at the top of the house.

He then marked off a space about 75 centimetres from the end wall.

"This is where the false wall will come," he explained. "I cannot make the room any bigger, but several people will be able to get in."

During the next few days, a number of "customers" came to the shop, each bringing tools and materials hidden in harmless-looking bags or boxes.

When it was finished, not even Corrie could have guessed that there was anything behind that stained old wall, with a bookcase against it. None of it looked new. Somehow the workmen had made the new wall look a hundred years old! Mr Smit was very pleased with the result.

"They will never find this," he said. "But now you must practise getting your 'guests' in there in the shortest possible time. And they must leave nothing behind in the house to show that they are here. If they are eating a meal, their cups and plates must be hidden. If it is at night, even the mattresses on their beds must be turned over so that there is no 'warm spot' for the Gestapo to find."

By now they had four regular guests and often other members of the underground as well. So there had to be many practices. In the end they managed it in just over a minute.

To give them a little time, one of the guests fixed up an alarm system with a buzzer and several push-buttons, including one near the door of the shop.

Danger

As far as possible Corrie tried to find other houses where the Jews could hide. A farm in the country, or a big house,

Corrie at the entrance to the secret room

was much safer than her family's little shop in the centre of Haarlem.

By now she was in touch with about eighty people, all helping the Jews to escape. Some were only teenagers who ran messages. Usually they used a code.

"We have an old watch, with an unusual face. Do you know someone who would like to buy it?" This would mean that there was an elderly Jew whose face would easily give him away.

One day a policeman named Rolf came into the watch shop. Corrie knew he was one of the underground workers. He asked Corrie if she could send a messenger to another house with a warning that the Germans were planning to raid it.

A boy of seventeen named Jop volunteered to go. But unfortunately the Gestapo got to the house first, and Jop was caught. Corrie and her friends knew that Jop would be tortured. It would be hard for him not to give anything away.

The ten Boom family knew that they ought to stop their work for the Jews now, before they also were arrested. But how could they let their Jewish friends down? They had to go on.

Arrested

It happened one Wednesday morning in February 1944. Corrie was ill with flu at the time. A Dutchman whom Corrie did not know asked for some money. He said he needed it urgently to save some Jews. Corrie did not feel sure about him, but could not risk letting down any Jews. It turned out later that the Dutchman was working for the Germans.

She went back to bed because she was so unwell. Suddenly the buzzer sounded. All the guests piled into the secret room.

Some Gestapo officers and two Dutch Nazis burst into the house. They took all the ten Boom family into the living-room. Corrie's brother Willem happened to be in the house that day, as well as some Dutch people who knew nothing about the Jews.

One of the Gestapo took Corrie into another room.

"Where are the Jews?" he asked.

"There aren't any Jews here," answered Corrie. She hated telling lies, but surely that was better than allowing people to be murdered, she thought.

The policeman hit her, repeating the question, but Corrie did not answer.

"Where is the secret room, then?" he asked, keeping on at her and hitting her again and again. Corrie felt blood in her mouth. She was so ill, and felt faint.

"Lord Jesus, help me," she cried out.

"If you use that name again, I'll kill you," said the policeman. But he stopped beating her and took her back to the others.

Next he started on Betsie. When she came back she also was bruised and bleeding.

All this time, German soldiers were searching the house, smashing open cupboards and doors in an effort to find the secret room. But they could not find it, and after half an hour they gave up.

"All right," said the officer in charge, "take this lot to the police station, and set a guard outside the house. If anyone is here, they'll starve to death."

At the police station, Corrie and her family had to spend the rest of the day sitting on the floor of a large room. Many other people had been arrested at the same time, including Pickwick.

The Dutch policeman named Rolf came into the room.

"Let's have it quiet in here," he shouted. "Toilets are outside at the back. You may go out one at a time under escort."

Then he bent down quickly and whispered in Willem's ear, "You can tear up any papers you don't want the police to see, and flush them down the toilet." Willem passed this on to the others who needed to know.

At home, every evening at about nine o'clock Father ten

The ten Boom family at the beginning of the war (Corrie and Father ten Boom sitting, Betsie standing on the right)

Boom always held family prayers. Here, under arrest, a group gathered round him to do the same. There was no Bible, but Father ten Boom knew much of it by heart anyway. In his deep voice he quoted some words from Psalm 119:

"Thou art my hiding place and my shield: I hope in thy word.... Hold thou me up, and I shall be safe."

His faith in God gave the others comfort and strength.

Life in prison

The next day they were taken to a prison near The Hague, a town 40 kilometres south of Haarlem. Each prisoner from Haarlem was put in a different cell. The last time they saw Father ten Boom was when they were led to their cells. Ten days later he died.

At first Corrie was put in a cell with several other women.

However, when it was discovered that she was ill, she was taken under guard to see a doctor at a hospital.

The Dutch doctor said she was seriously ill, hoping the police would allow her to stay in the hospital. But instead they took her back to the prison and put her in a cell by herself. She stayed there for four months.

Before she left the hospital a nurse had given Corrie a small packet, which she hid in her clothes. In it she found a toothbrush, some soap and, best of all, copies of the four Gospels in booklet form.

Life in prison is never pleasant, but here it was dreadful. There was no bed in Corrie's cell, just a dirty straw mattress with only one blanket, which someone had been sick on. The cell was bitterly cold. The only food was a plate of thin porridge each morning, and one piece of black bread in the evening.

At first Corrie was very ill, but gradually her strength returned. She desperately wanted to talk to someone, but the women warders were very strict. Even the "trusty" prisoners who brought the food round were afraid to talk to her.

Every day Corrie wondered what had happened to the other prisoners from Haarlem. One day the chance came to find out. All the prisoners started to make a noise and the warders did not stop them. It was Hitler's birthday, and all the warders were at a party!

The prisoners called out their names to each other, and passed on all the news they could. Corrie learned that most of the people from Haarlem had been released. Her sister Betsie was still in prison, and there was no news of her father. It was only later that she heard he had died.

One day when Corrie was a little better, a warder threw a parcel into her cell. She was thrilled to find that it contained some biscuits, a bright-red towel and a needle and thread. It had come from her married sister Nollie, who lived in Haarlem.

She noticed there was something odd about the address and the stamp. It was all crooked. Suddenly she had an idea, and peeled off the stamp. There was some writing underneath: "All the watches left in the cupboard are safe." This meant that all the Jews hiding in the ten Boom home had escaped. That was wonderful news.

The hearing

However, there was still the hearing to come, when Corrie would be questioned by a Gestapo officer. This could be terrible. Torture was often used to gain information. Every prisoner was afraid that they might give some of their friends away.

Corrie was called for her hearing one chilly morning in May.

"Lord Jesus," she prayed, "you were once questioned too. Please show me what to do."

The German officer began in a very friendly way.

"I would like to help you, Miss ten Boom. But you must tell me everything."

Corrie and her co-workers in the underground had often practised answering questions. For an hour the German officer questioned her, and she managed to avoid giving away anything vital. He specially wanted to know how the ration cards had been stolen. Corrie was glad she really did not know!

"And now tell me about your other activities, Miss ten Boom."

"Other activities? Oh yes, about the girls' clubs and my work for the mentally handicapped."

Of course, the German officer did not mean this, but Corrie eagerly told him all about it, and he listened in amazement.

"But that is a waste of time," he said.

"Oh no," said Corrie. "God loves everyone, even the weak and feeble. You see, the Bible tells us that God looks at things very differently from us."

"That will be enough for today," the officer snapped.

But the next day, when the hearing continued, the officer asked Corrie more and more about God and the Bible. It turned out that he hated the work he had to do. Also he was very worried about his family in Germany, because their town was being bombed every night. Corrie was able to tell him about the peace and forgiveness which Jesus Christ can give if we ask Him.

From then on, the officer actually helped Corrie all he could. He gave her a chance to see her relations when her father's will was read out. But he did not have the power to set Corrie or Betsie free.

All this time, Corrie was still in a cell on her own. It was terribly lonely. But she had one friend – an ant! She gave it a few crumbs of bread whenever it appeared from a crack in the floor.

During the four months that Corrie was alone in her cell, she spent much of her time reading and re-reading the four Gospels that the hospital nurse had given her. The life and suffering of Jesus became more real to her than ever before. She even began to see that all her suffering might have a purpose. The death of Jesus had brought forgiveness to mankind. In the same way, she felt that God can bring something good out of troubles that we go through. This thought gave her fresh courage and strength.

One day in June 1944, all the prisoners were told to pack their belongings. They were marched to the railway station and put on a train. As they were getting into the train, Corrie saw her sister Betsie, and managed to push her way through the crowd to reach her. At last they were together again.

The train took them to a labour camp in southern Holland. Here they lived in barracks. During the day they had to work. Corrie was put in a section of the Philips factory, making radios for German aircraft. She took care to make plenty of mistakes!

Life was still hard. Punishments were very severe, and sometimes men prisoners were shot. But everyone knew that the Allies had now invaded Europe, so that there was hope at last.

By September there were rumours that the Allied army was not far from Holland. One day the prisoners heard a lot of explosions and they became very excited. But it turned out that the Germans had only been blowing up roads and bridges.

The next day, the Germans shot 700 of the men prisoners. The women and the rest of the men were put into cattle trucks and sent to Germany.

Ravensbruck

Corrie and Betsie were taken to Ravensbruck concentration camp. This was worse than any other prison they had been in. The first two days they had to sleep out in the open. It poured with rain, and the ground became a sea of mud. Then they were packed into a huge barrack-room. It had been built to house 400 people, but there were now 1400 prisoners in it. They had to sleep on straw mattresses filled with choking dust and swarming with fleas. Even the guards did not like going into the barrack-room because of the fleas.

The barrack-room at Ravensbruck concentration camp (still from The Hiding Place)

Roll-call was at half-past four in the morning. There were 35 000 women in the camp, and if anyone was missing they were counted again and again. So it often went on for hours. If the prisoners did not stand up straight the women guards beat them with riding-whips.

The work was extremely hard. Corrie and Betsie had to load heavy sheets of steel on to carts, push them for a certain distance, then unload them. All the time the guards shouted at them to work faster.

They were only given a potato and some thin soup at lunch-time, and some turnip soup with a piece of black bread in the evening. The prisoners who were doing lighter work had no lunch at all.

If the prisoners became ill, the guards took no notice of them unless their temperature was over 40°C, which meant they were very seriously ill. Then they had to join the long queue for the camp hospital. But nothing was done for them when they finally got there. When the hospital was full, the weakest prisoners were put on lorries and taken to gas chambers to be killed. Then their bodies were burned. The tall chimney above the ovens in the centre of the camp was always belching grey smoke.

This was the "hell on earth" to which Corrie and Betsie had come. Yet when they arrived at Ravensbruck, God had shown them that He could still help them, even in a place as terrible as this.

Before they left Holland, on the day Father ten Boom's will had been read, one of Corrie's relations had managed to smuggle a small Bible to her. She had also received a bottle of vitamin drops in one of the parcels sent to prisoners by the Red Cross. When the prisoners arrived at Ravensbruck they had to give up everything they had with them. Corrie was determined to keep the Bible and the vitamin drops. Somehow she managed to smuggle them in without a guard seeing them.

When they first moved into the barrack-room, the conditions there had made the women angry and selfish. There were arguments and fights. Everyone suffered so much that they spent all their energy looking after themselves.

When Betsie noticed this, she began to pray that God would bring peace to the barrack-room. Very soon the atmosphere changed. The women became a little more patient with each other. They even began to make a few jokes about their troubles.

In the evenings, after a hard day's work and a miserable supper, Corrie and Betsie took out the little Dutch Bible.

At first a small group gathered round to listen, then more and more women joined them. The guards never came in to stop them, because of the fleas. So Corrie and Betsie thanked God for the fleas!

The women came from many countries, including Poland, France, Germany and Russia. Corrie translated the Bible from Dutch into German, someone else translated the German into Polish, and so on.

Under these terrible conditions, the goodness in the words of the Bible shone out brightly and their message of God's love brought comfort. With death all around, the promise of eternal life and the glory of heaven gave the women hope for the future.

One day, Betsie was cruelly whipped by a guard for not working hard enough. But she did not give in to hatred. She prayed for the guards as much as she prayed for the prisoners. Corrie found this very difficult, but somehow Betsie seemed to have risen above all the suffering, and to be living very close to God.

One night as they were lying on their bunks, Betsie whispered to Corrie, "I can see a house, somewhere in Holland. It is a beautiful house with a large garden. There is a large hall with a carved wooden staircase. We are going to look after people who have been hurt in the war, until they can live a normal life again. Corrie, I believe God is going to give us a house like this."

Later on, Betsie had another vision. This time she saw a concentration camp in Germany. But there was no barbed wire in this camp, and there were no guards. All the buildings were painted a cheerful green. It was a camp for German people who had been hurt by the evil of Hitler, even people like the guards at Ravensbruck, who had been taught to be so cruel.

"Corrie," she said, "we must tell people how good God

is. After the war we must go round the world telling people. No one will be able to say they have suffered worse than us. We can tell them how wonderful God is, and how His love will fill our lives, if only we will give up our hatred and bitterness."

All this time Corrie had been giving Betsie a few vitamin drops each day because she was so weak. But there were so many other needy prisoners that she began giving drops to them also. She gave them to more and more people. She knew the bottle must soon be empty. But every day more drops came. Nobody could understand it, until Betsie reminded them of the story in the Bible of the widow's jar of oil, which did not run dry for many days.

Gradually, however, Betsie became weaker and weaker. It was bitterly cold, for it was now November. In the end, Betsie was so ill that she was admitted to the hospital. Corrie was not allowed to visit her sister, but each day went to look at her through one of the hospital windows. Finally, one day Betsie's bed was empty.

Corrie was heart-broken. At first she did not dare to look in the room where the dead were placed. Then another prisoner called her. There was Betsie. Yes, she was dead. But her face had changed. Instead of being full of pain and suffering as it had been, it was now beautiful, like the face of an angel!

Death or freedom?

Once again it was roll-call. The women stamped their feet to keep warm. Suddenly Corrie heard her name: "Prisoner ten Boom, report after roll-call."

What was going to happen? Was she going to be punished? Or shot?

"Father in heaven, please help me now," she prayed.

When she reported, she was given a card stamped "Ent-lassen", which means "Released". She was free! She could hardly believe it. She was given back her few possessions, some new clothes and a railway pass back to Holland. After a long, hard journey, she arrived back among friends in her own country.

Afterwards she learned that she had been released by mistake. A week after her release all the women of her age in the camp were killed.

Sharing the good news

As soon as she was well enough, Corrie began to tell of her experiences. When the war ended a few months later, she told people about Betsie's vision of a house for people who had suffered during the war. One person who heard it was a lady whose son had returned from prison in Germany. She was so grateful to God that she gave her large house to Corrie for this work. It was just the kind of house that Betsie had seen in her vision!

In that house many people found peace and comfort through the loving care that Corrie and others gave them.

After a while, news of Corrie's experiences reached other countries. She was invited to speak in America, England and many other countries. The hardest place for her to go was Germany, with all its bitter memories. But God helped her to love and to forgive, even when she met some of the former guards from Ravensbruck.

Then a Christian relief organisation in Germany asked her to help run a camp for refugees and people who had been made bitter by their experiences of life under Hitler. It turned out to be just like the concentration camp Betsie had seen in her vision! Again Corrie passed on the message of God's love and forgiveness.

22

Corrie on her travels

Corrie visiting prisoners in the Philippines

Corrie also wrote several books about her experiences. As a result, she received many more invitations to speak. For over thirty years Corrie visited country after country telling bitter, sad people how wonderful God is, just as Betsie had foretold. She went to nearly every country in the world, including Russia and other communist countries. Sometimes she travelled with Brother Andrew, another famous Dutch Christian.

Wherever Corrie went she tried to visit people in prison. She knew just how they felt. She had spent four months alone in a cell. She had been beaten. People she loved had been cruelly treated; some had been killed. But she also knew that God can take away all feelings of bitterness and hatred.

Corrie wrote down her story in a book called *The Hiding Place*, which was later made into a film of the same name. She also wrote several other books telling of her life before the war and her experiences travelling around the world.

Finally Corrie became too old to travel. In 1977 she settled down in a beautiful, peaceful home in America, where she continued to do all she could to share God's goodness with other people. Later she had a stroke and could no longer speak, but she was still full of the peace of God and prayed for people who wrote to her or visited her. Finally, on the evening of her ninety-first birthday, she died.

BIOGRAPHICAL NOTES

Corrie (short for Cornelia) ten Boom was born in Haarlem in Holland on 15 April 1892. The youngest child of Caspar and Cornelia ten Boom, she had two sisters, Betsie and Nollie, and a brother, Willem. Caspar ten Boom was a watchmaker. When Corrie grew up she became the first woman in Holland to qualify as a watchmaker.

Corrie ran the Haarlem Girls' Clubs from about 1921 to 1940. She also founded a Christian organisation for girls which at one time had thousands of members in Holland and Indonesia.

On 10 May 1940 German forces invaded Holland. Soon after this, the ten Boom family began their underground work, helping Jews to escape from the Germans.

On 28 February 1944 the ten Booms were arrested. Corrie's father was then 84. He died ten days after his arrest.

Corrie was taken to a prison at Scheveningen, near The Hague, along with Betsie and Willem. Willem was soon released, but died shortly after the war from an illness contracted in prison.

In June 1944 Corrie and Betsie were moved to a labour camp at Vught in southern Holland. In the same month the Allied forces invaded Europe and the last stage of the Second World War began.

In September 1944 the sisters were moved to Ravensbruck concentration camp in Germany. Betsie died there a few days before Christmas 1944. Corrie was released on 31 December 1944. Willem's son Kik died as prisoner of the Germans during the last few months of the war.

Holland was liberated by the Allies on 5 May 1945 and Germany surrendered on 8 May 1945.

Schapenduinen, the large house in Bloemendaal given to Corrie for her rehabilitation work, was opened in June 1945.

After the war Corrie was invited to speak in many countries. She visited over sixty countries, and came to Britain six times.

In 1968 she was honoured by the State of Israel for her work in aid of the Jews by being invited to plant a tree in the Avenue of the Righteous Gentiles, near Jerusalem.

In 1975 *The Hiding Place*, a film of Corrie's life, was released. In 1977 she finally gave up travelling and settled in California, where she died on 15 April 1983, her ninety-first birthday.

THINGS TO DO

A Test yourself

Here are some short questions. See if you can remember the answers from what you have read. Then write them down in a few words.

1 What was the name of the town in Holland where Corrie lived?

2 How many Jews in Europe were murdered by the Nazis?

3 How long did it take for the people in Corrie's home to hide in the secret room?

4 What did Corrie cry out when the Gestapo man kept on hitting her?

5 What did Father ten Boom do each evening at nine o'clock?

6 What was the message under the stamp on the parcel?

7 What "friend" did Corrie have when she was alone in her prison cell?

8 How many women were there in Ravensbruck concentration camp?

9 Why did the guards not stop the women reading their Bible in the barrack-room?

10 What is the title of the book and the film of Corrie's life?

B Think through

These questions need longer answers. Think about them, and then try to write two or three sentences in answer to each one. You may look up the story again to help you.

1 How did the lives of the people of Haarlem change when the Germans took over their country?

2 Why were Corrie and her family so concerned about the Jews?

3 Why did the German officer in the prison want to know more about God and the Bible?

4 How did it help Corrie to read about the life of Jesus while she was alone in prison?

5 How could the story in the Bible of the widow and the jar of oil (1 Kings, chapter 17, verses 7–16) explain why Corrie's vitamin bottle lasted so long?

6 What was the message that Betsie felt they must tell other people after the war?

C Talk about

Here are some questions for you to discuss together. Try to give reasons for what you say or think. Try to find out all the different opinions which people have about each question.

1 Can you think of any reasons why the Jews have been persecuted so often? Why did Hitler want to wipe them out? Why are many Jews and Christians having difficulties in Russia today? Is it anything to do with their being God's people?

2 Why did God allow Corrie and her family to be arrested? Did anything good come out of it?

3 How do you explain Betsie's visions and the way they came true? Is it possible for people to live so close to God that He can show them things that He wants them to know about their future work for Him? (Compare Paul's vision in Acts, chapter 16, verses 9–10.)

D Find out

Choose one or two of the subjects below and find out all you can about them. History books, geography books and encyclopaedias may be useful. You could also use reference books in your school or public library to look up some of the people and organisations.

1 *The Jews*

(a) How did the Jewish nation begin? Using a Bible, write a short account of the part played by each of the following people:

Abraham (Genesis, chapters 12–25)
Moses (Exodus, chapters 2–20)
King David (1 Samuel, chapters 16–17; 2 Samuel, chapters 5–8)
Queen Esther (The Book of Esther)

(b) Find out about the Zionist movement, the persecution of the Jews under Hitler and the founding of the State of Israel in 1948. You can write to the Board of Deputies of British Jews (see p. 29) for information.

(c) Learn all you can about the modern State of Israel. The Information Department at the Embassy of Israel (see p. 29) will be able to help you.

(d) How do Jews worship? What is a synagogue, and a rabbi? What do Jews believe about Jesus?

2 *Youth work*
   (a) Make a list of the youth clubs in your area. Find out whether they are run by a church, the local council or a voluntary organisation.
   (b) Find out about one or more national youth organisations such as the Girl Guides, Boys' Brigade and Scouts. Find out how they started, how they are organised and what their aims are.

3 *Mentally handicapped people*
   (a) What are mentally handicapped people? What are some of the causes for people being born like this, or becoming like this?
   (b) How can we help mentally handicapped people? You can contact the National Society for the Mentally Handicapped (see p. 29) for information.

4 *Nazi Germany*
   (a) Who was Hitler, and how did he come to power in Germany?
   (b) What did Hitler believe about the German people and other members of the "Aryan" race? What did he believe about other races?
   (c) What was the Nazi Party? What is a dictator?
   (d) Find out about Sir Oswald Mosley and the "blackshirt" movement in Britain before the war.

5 *Resistance movements*
   Find out about the underground resistance movements in Europe during the Second World War. Books about the television series *The Secret Army* (see p. 29) will help you. Look for other books on the subject in your library. Try to find out about Violet Szabo and Odette Churchill (see p. 29), British women who worked with the French resistance movement.

USEFUL INFORMATION

Addresses

The Education Department
The Board of Deputies of
 British Jews
Woburn House
Upper Woburn Place
London WC1H 0EP.

The Information Department
 Embassy of Israel
2 Palace Green
London W8 4QB

The Information Department
MENCAP
123 Golden Lane
London EC1Y 0RT.

N.B. It is best if only one person in each class writes off for information. Remember to enclose a stamped, addressed envelope for the reply. A postal order for 50p would also be helpful, if you want plenty of material.

More books to read

Bible Smuggler: Brother Andrew, by David Wallington (R.E.P.) (P).
Corrie, by Kathleen White (Marshall & Pickering) (T/P).
Corrie – The Lives She's Touched, by Joan Winmill Brown (Hodder & Stoughton) (T/P).
The Diary of Anne Frank, (Pan Books) (T).
The Hiding Place, by Corrie ten Boom (Hodder & Stoughton) (T).
In My Father's House, by Corrie ten Boom (Hodder & Stoughton) (T).
Odette, by Gerrard Tickell (Kay & Ward) (T).
The Secret Army, by John Brason (W. H. Allen) (T).
Tramp for the Lord, by Corrie ten Boom (Hodder & Stoughton) (T).

(T) = suitable for teachers and older pupils
(P) = suitable for younger pupils

Films and videos

The Hiding Place (160 min), colour. A full-length feature film about Corrie ten Boom's wartime experiences. Available from International Films Ltd, 235 Shaftesbury Avenue, London WC2 8EL. Also available in video from Christian Video Experience, 6 Cecil Way, Hayes, nr Bromley, Kent BR2 7JU.

Behind the Hiding Place (60 min), colour. A film about the making of *The Hiding Place* (above). Available from International Films Ltd. Also available in video from Christian Video Experience.

Corrie – The Lives She's Touched (90 min), colour. Shows some of the people whose lives have been changed by meeting Corrie ten Boom. Available from International Films Ltd.